Laubach Way to Reading

DIAGNOSTIC INVENTORY
Teacher's Manual

Diane J. Sawyer, Ph.D.
Syracuse University
Syracuse, New York

Craig Dougherty, Ph.D.
Dougherty Associates
Fulton, New York

Sally Lipa, Ph.D.
State University College
Geneseo, New York

NEW READERS PRESS
Publishing Division of Laubach Literacy International
Syracuse, New York

Acknowledgments

The publisher gratefully acknowledges the contributions of local Laubach Literacy Action groups who field-tested the LWR Diagnostic Inventory, of the programs staff at Laubach Literacy International, who evaluated the material throughout its development, and of Allen Manning, Ph.D., who initiated the project and coordinated the field-testing.

ISBN 0-88336-979-X

© 1987, 1991

New Readers Press
Publishing Division of Laubach Literacy International
Box 131, Syracuse, NY 13210

Edited by Kay Koschnick
Designed by Chris Steenwerth
Printed in the United States of America

20 19 18 17 16 15 14 13 12 11
10   9   8   7   6   5   4   3   2   1

About the Authors

Diane J. Sawyer is director of the Reading Clinic at Syracuse University and has been involved in the assessment of reading performance for more than 20 years. She has been a classroom teacher and a school reading specialist and has taught courses in the diagnosis and remediation of reading difficulties at both the undergraduate and graduate levels. She has written numerous articles on the subject and is a frequent presenter at national and international conferences on reading. Her research interests focus on the relationship between language and reading acquisition. In pursuit of this interest, she has worked with new readers of all ages in the United States and abroad. Since 1982, Dr. Sawyer has been Test Review Coordinator for the journals of the International Reading Association.

Craig Dougherty received his B.A. from Muhlenberg College in 1971 and held a variety of public school positions over a 10-year period. After earning his M.S. in 1975 from Syracuse University, he became affiliated with the Syracuse University Reading Clinic and began working with adult learners. He was director of the clinic reading program for developmentally delayed adults. He has conducted workshops and presented papers on adult reading disabilities. He received his Ph.D. in 1981 and has been conducting research in the area of reading acquisition and comprehension since that time. He has also been involved in developing materials for measuring reading ability and aptitude.

Sally Lipa earned her doctorate in reading education from Syracuse University in 1977. She is presently an associate professor of reading education at the State University College at Geneseo, New York. There she teaches undergraduate and graduate courses in reading education and directs the reading clinic. She has presented numerous papers on the nature of reading disability, on diagnostic assessment, and on remedial techniques.

Table of Contents

Introduction

The Laubach Way to Reading Diagnostic Inventory reflects reading skills taught in the four skill books of the Laubach Way to Reading (LWR) series.

This basic series, designed for adults, offers systematic instruction in the sounds and structure of words, word meanings, reading comprehension, and writing practice. Material increases in difficulty and complexity as a student progresses from *Skill Book 1* through *Skill Book 4*.

To make the best use of time for learning and teaching basic skills, it is very helpful to determine what a new student already knows about reading. When this is established, instruction and learning may begin at an appropriate level, and the teacher or tutor has guidance as to which skill areas to stress with the particular student.

Purpose of Diagnostic Inventory

The LWR Diagnostic Inventory is an aid for people teaching basic reading to adults. It is of particular use to those using the Laubach Way to Reading series since the sequence of skills follows that of LWR and since suggestions for remediation are keyed to LWR.

The purpose of the LWR Diagnostic Inventory is both to place students in the appropriate skill book in the LWR series and to give the teacher a fairly detailed record of a student's present reading skills. By profiling a student's strengths and weaknesses in reading, the diagnostic inventory alerts a teacher to the skills which probably ought to receive special emphasis during lessons and to the skills which may only require relatively short periods of time for learning.

Steps in Administering the LWR Diagnostic Inventory

1. **Administer the LWR Screening Lists.** This consists of four fairly short word lists, one list for each level of the LWR series. It will give a rough indication of the appropriate skill book level for the student.

There are three items you will need:

a. The LWR Screening Lists, from which the student will read.

b. The LWR Screening Lists Record Sheet, on which you will record the student's correct answers as he gives them.

c. Directions for giving the LWR Screening Lists, found in Part 1 of this manual.

The LWR Screening Lists and the accompanying LWR Screening Lists Record Sheet are each a single sheet. They are given in Part 1 of this manual as blackline masters, from which you may make photocopies. Make the appropriate number of copies for all students being placed in LWR. One copy of the LWR Screening Lists sheet can be used over and over again, but you will need a copy of the LWR Screening Lists Record Sheet for each student.

A chart given both in this manual and on the LWR Screening Lists Record Sheet tells how to use the results to determine which Student Reading Profile the student should take.

2. **Administer the appropriate Student Reading Profile.** There are four Student Reading Profile booklets. Each reflects the major phonics, word analysis, comprehension, and writing skills taught in one of the four LWR skill books. Part 2 of this manual explains how to administer and score the Student Reading Profile booklet.

3. **Place the student in the appropriate skill book.** Consult Part 3 of this manual for information on placement. The person who administers the Student Reading Profile may also fill out the Checklist of Skills to Emphasize given in Part 3. This will provide a summary for the tutor of the skills that need special attention. The Checklist is given as a blackline master which you may photocopy.

4. **Learning and teaching take place.** As you are teaching, refer to the Checklist of Skills to Emphasize and to Part 4 of this manual, which recommends exercises and materials to help with skill areas in which the student needs extra work.

Administering the LWR Diagnostic Inventory:
Summary of Steps

1. Administer the LWR Screening Lists.
(See Part 1 of manual.)

Place student in one of the four Student Reading Profiles.
(See Part 1 of manual.)

2. Administer the appropriate Student Reading Profile booklet.
(See Part 2 of manual.)

3. Place student in the appropriate LWR skill book.
(See Part 3 of manual.)

Person who administered Student Reading Profile fills out
the Checklist of Skills to Emphasize for the tutor's use.
(See Part 3 of manual.)

4. Learning and teaching take place.
Refer to the Checklist of Skills to Emphasize.
(See Part 4 of manual for recommended activities and materials
in skill areas in which student needs extra work.)

Time Needed to Administer

The amount of time needed to administer the LWR Diagnostic Inventory—including both the Screening Lists and a Student Reading Profile—varies with the particular student. In general, allow up to 15 or 20 minutes for the Screening Lists if the student goes through all four of them. Another hour to an hour and a half should be allowed for the Student Reading Profile.

Ways to Administer
the LWR Diagnostic Inventory

In either an adult basic education center or a volunteer literacy center, there are three possible ways to administer the LWR Diagnostic Inventory:

1. A staff intake person administers both the Screening Lists and the appropriate Student Reading Profile to the student at the same session. This person also fills out the Checklist of Skills to Emphasize for the tutor's use. The results should be available to the tutor before the first teaching session with the student.

2. A staff intake person administers the Screening Lists. The tutor or teacher administers the appropriate Student Reading Profile during the first session or sessions with the student.

3. The tutor or teacher administers both the Screening Lists and the appropriate Student Reading Profile. The Screening Lists may be done at the first session. The appropriate Student Reading Profile may be completed during the same first session or during the first few sessions.

Once the Student Reading Profile is completed and scored, the tutor may refer to the Checklist of Skills to Emphasize and to Part 4 of this manual for ideas on using LWR to the best advantage for the particular student.

Helping Your Student Feel Calm

Many people experience anxiety when their skills are to be evaluated. This tends to be especially true for adult low-level readers. As you work through these materials with your student, do all you can to ease whatever anxiety he or she may be feeling. Here are some suggestions on how to do this.

1. Provide a calm, warm, accepting, reassuring atmosphere for your student. If you are relaxed, your student will relax and feel less anxious.

2. Begin by talking about something totally non-threatening (the weather, for example). A few minutes of this is enough, however. In general, students appreciate it when you stay on task.

3. Avoid referring to any part of the LWR Diagnostic Inventory as a "test." It isn't a test in the sense that most students remember tests. That is, your student won't be compared with other students, and there is no question of passing or failing.

Emphasize that the purpose is to get a profile, or picture, of where the student is in reading. With the help of this picture, you will be able to give lessons that are at the right level for the student: not too difficult, and not too easy.

Explain that although the process takes an hour or two away from a regular lesson, in the long run it will save time. This is because, with the results, you will be able to move quickly over things the student already knows. And you will know when extra time and activities will probably be needed. So the Diagnostic Inventory will allow you to be more in tune with the student's present reading skills and will thus help you give lessons that meet the particular needs of the student.

4. Part of the anxiety about being evaluated comes from fear of making mistakes. Many students, after years of experience, have decided that making mistakes is painful. And the strategy they've come to rely on is one of avoiding situations in which they might make mistakes.

Reassure your student that in the Laubach method, mistakes are a natural part of learning. A mistake is nothing but a signal that something hasn't been learned *yet*. In any learning situation—learning to repair cars, learning to cook, or whatever—mistakes give the learner useful information. They tell what still needs to be learned. In the Laubach method, mistakes are *valued* because they give both teacher and student a sense of what to work on.

5. As you work through the Diagnostic Inventory with the student, be very open in discussing the process. When you discover something interesting, share the discovery with the student. Make the student a partner in the process.

6. The Diagnostic Inventory is designed to help you attune yourself to the student. Look for additional ways of doing this. For example, at some point early in your teaching, begin trying to get a sense of your particular student's learning style. As you give the Diagnostic Inventory, and as you begin LWR, observe what sorts of activities and interactions seem to help your student feel both calm and interested. Make adjustments when something upsets the student.

Also, some useful things to ask about are: What school experiences that you can remember were really helpful? What teacher or tutor that you remember was good at helping you learn? What did that person do that worked well? Answers to these questions might give you some useful ideas about ways of working with your student.

An Important Tip

As you administer the LWR Screening Lists and the Student Reading Profiles, explain to the student that you will not be telling him whether his answer is right or not as you go along. When the student answers an item orally, make some noncommittal response to indicate that you heard him, such as: "Thank you. Go on to number 6." Be very careful not to give any positive or negative feedback about the student's answer in anything you say or do.

Skills Assessment and the Teacher's Craft

The LWR Screening Lists are designed to give you a rough indication of where in the LWR series a particular student should begin. The LWR Student Reading Profiles are designed to validate and refine that placement and to give you a sense of what a particular student's present reading skills are.

But, as with all tools which sample skills, the best one can claim for these tools is that they are *generally* accurate. Chances are that they will be fairly accurate for your particular student, but there can be no absolute guarantee of that.

And so, you will need to use some common sense as you work with these tools. If, after you start your student somewhere in LWR, you discover that he or she lacks certain important prerequisite skills, then make adjustments.

Here's an example. The LWR Screening Lists might place your student in Student Reading Profile 2. Your student completes Student Reading Profile 2, and you get a sense of his or her present reading skills. You begin teaching in *Skill Book 2*. After a lesson or two, you realize that your student hasn't yet learned to identify two initial consonant sounds taught in *Skill Book 1*. Still, except for that problem, you feel that *Skill Book 2* is at the right level for your student.

So, rather than take your student all the way through *Skill Book 1*, you just go back and teach the particular initial consonant sounds the student needs to learn. To find appropriate material, you can refer to the charts titled "Skills Introduced in Skill Book 1" at the front of the *Teacher's Manual for Skill Book 1*. This chart will show all of the places where a particular skill is taught either in the skill book itself or in exercises that appear only in the teacher's manual.

You can also go to Part 4 of this manual, which will tell you where to go in LWR for help and will also suggest activities you may use to teach the particular skill.

The point is that your student's scores in these materials will give you useful information about his or her present reading skills. But you should also be alert for gaps in your student's skills which the LWR Diagnostic Inventory fails to uncover. Then respond to your student's needs accordingly. This sort of flexibility and sensitivity is part of the teacher's craft. The Screening Lists and the Student Reading Profiles are good tools. But, as with good carpenter's tools, it still takes care to get a good result.

— Part 1 —
Screening

How to Administer the LWR Screening Lists

You will need a copy of the Screening Lists (one sheet) for the student to read from and a copy of the Screening Lists Record Sheet (one sheet) for you to record the student's correct answers and his total score. Both of these items appear in this manual as blackline masters from which you may make photocopies.

You may want to fold the Screening Lists sheet lengthwise so that only one list appears at a time. Or you may use a blank piece of paper to cover all but List 1 when S. begins.

> T: In a moment, I am going to ask you to read some words. The purpose is to find out where you are in your reading. That way, we can work at a level that's right for you.

> T: Look at the first list. Read each word you know. If you aren't sure you know a word, say what you think it might be, or just say, "I don't know." Then go on to the next word.

Check (✓) each word that S. reads correctly. If S. misses four words in a row on any list, stop at that point.

When S. has finished a list—or if you have stopped him—record the total correct for that list. (If you stopped him, record the total correct before you stopped.)

If S. scored at mastery level for a list, go on to the next list. If S. scored at less than mastery level, see the chart below. (This chart appears also on the Record Sheet for your convenience.)

Note: No matter where S. finishes on the lists, compliment S. on his or her effort and be supportive.

The chart below explains how to use a student's LWR Screening Lists score.

List 1:	9-10	— Go on to List 2.
	0-8	— Administer Student Reading Profile 1.
List 2:	13-15	— Go on to List 3.
	8-12	— Administer Student Reading Profile 2.
	0-7	— Administer Student Reading Profile 1.
List 3:	13-15	— Go on to List 4.
	8-12	— Administer Student Reading Profile 3.
	0-7	— Administer Student Reading Profile 2.
List 4:	13-20	— Administer Student Reading Profile 4.
	0-12	— Administer Student Reading Profile 3.

LWR Screening Lists

List 1	List 2	List 3	List 4
1. in	1. glass	1. cry	1. about
2. is	2. send	2. loaf	2. bought
3. the	3. dropped	3. die	3. shook
4. a	4. far	4. flight	4. gentle
5. to	5. running	5. eleven	5. cough
6. has	6. after	6. future	6. thumb
7. her	7. quick	7. menu	7. weigh
8. this	8. girls	8. money	8. schedule
9. she	9. then	9. retire	9. wrong
10. his	10. hurry	10. short	10. pressure
	11. which	11. snow	11. league
	12. were	12. table	12. excuse
	13. dishes	13. zero	13. annoy
	14. work	14. sleep	14. choose
	15. from	15. paint	15. ache
			16. crawl
			17. beautiful
			18. hour
			19. above
			20. argue

LWR Screening Lists Record Sheet

Student's name _____

Date _____   Person administering _____

List 1	List 2	List 3	List 4
_____ 1. in	_____ 1. glass	_____ 1. cry	_____ 1. about
_____ 2. is	_____ 2. send	_____ 2. loaf	_____ 2. bought
_____ 3. the	_____ 3. dropped	_____ 3. die	_____ 3. shook
_____ 4. a	_____ 4. far	_____ 4. flight	_____ 4. gentle
_____ 5. to	_____ 5. running	_____ 5. eleven	_____ 5. cough
_____ 6. has	_____ 6. after	_____ 6. future	_____ 6. thumb
_____ 7. her	_____ 7. quick	_____ 7. menu	_____ 7. weigh
_____ 8. this	_____ 8. girls	_____ 8. money	_____ 8. schedule
_____ 9. she	_____ 9. then	_____ 9. retire	_____ 9. wrong
_____ 10. his	_____ 10. hurry	_____ 10. short	_____ 10. pressure
	_____ 11. which	_____ 11. snow	_____ 11. league
	_____ 12. were	_____ 12. table	_____ 12. excuse
	_____ 13. dishes	_____ 13. zero	_____ 13. annoy
	_____ 14. work	_____ 14. sleep	_____ 14. choose
	_____ 15. from	_____ 15. paint	_____ 15. ache
			_____ 16. crawl
			_____ 17. beautiful
			_____ 18. hour
			_____ 19. above
			_____ 20. argue

Total Correct: ____ / 10	Total Correct: ____ / 15	Total Correct: ____ / 15	Total Correct: ____ / 20
Mastery Level: 9/10	Mastery Level: 13/15	Mastery Level: 13/15	Mastery Level: 18/20

The chart below explains how to use a student's LWR Screening Lists score.

List 1:   9-10 — Go on to List 2.
             0-8 — Administer Student Reading Profile 1.

List 2:   13-15 — Go on to List 3.
             8-12 — Administer Student Reading Profile 2.
             0-7 — Administer Student Reading Profile 1.

List 3:   13-15 — Go on to List 4.
             8-12 — Administer Student Reading Profile 3.
             0-7 — Administer Student Reading Profile 2.

List 4:   13-20 — Administer Student Reading Profile 4.
             0-12 — Administer Student Reading Profile 3.

—— Part 2. ——
Administering the Student Reading Profiles

Administering Student Reading Profile 1

Student Reading Profile 1 reflects the instructional tasks included in *Skill Book 1* of the Laubach Way to Reading series. The seven parts in this Student Reading Profile are:

1. Segmentation
2. Auditory Discrimination
3. Sounds and Letters
4. Word Recognition
5. Writing
6. Parts of Written Language
7. Comprehension

All pages in the Student Reading Profile booklet are perforated. Before you begin, tear out the teacher's pages at the front. In this booklet, they are the first three sheets of paper (pages 1-6). These teacher's pages are marked with a black border at the top and bottom to help you identify them.

You will use the teacher's pages from the booklet for scoring the first sections of the reading profile while S. is answering questions. Teacher's page 2 is the Summary Record, which you will use at the end to record the student's total scores for all sections of the Student Reading Profile.

Before beginning, explain to S. that doing this Student Reading Profile should take an hour to an hour and a half. Be very warm and supportive throughout the process of giving this reading profile. If S. becomes overly frustrated by any section of the profile, stop and go on to the next section.

1. SEGMENTATION

Note: In section 1-A and in a number of sections in this Student Reading Profile, S. is given an example or two for practice. It may happen that S. will have difficulty producing a correct response for a particular practice item. If so, before beginning the regular items, take time to explain both the practice task and the correct response. If S. then *still* cannot perform the task, try one or two regular items. Move on to the next section if S. also misses these items.

1-A: Number of Words in a Sentence
(Teacher's page 3, no student page)

You will need seven coins, preferably all the same denomination, for this section. No other student material is needed. Place the seven coins in front of S., in a mass.

> T: I am going to say some sentences. Listen carefully. You are going to use one coin for each word in a sentence. For example, if I say, "Dick walked," you would use one coin for the word *Dick* and another coin for the word *walked*.

As you say *Dick walked*, place one coin for each word in front of S. Place the two coins in the student's left-right order.

> T: Repeat the sentence, and point to the coin that stands for each word.

S. should point to the first coin at the left and say, "Dick." Then S. should point to the second coin and say, "walked."

> T: That's right: *Dick walked*. This coin stands for *Dick*, and this coin stands for *walked*.

If S. had difficulty, place the seven coins together again, and use this second example:

> T: Let's try another sentence. Remember, you are to place coins in a row in front of you. Place one coin for each word in the sentence. Here is the sentence: *Mother works hard*. Use one coin for each word in the sentence I just said.

S. should place three coins in a row left to right.

> T: Say the sentence again, pointing to each coin that stands for a word.

S. should point to the three coins from left to right as if reading words in a sentence as he says, "Mother works hard."

Now read the following sentences, placing the seven coins together prior to reading each one. On the teacher's scoring page 3, put a check mark in the blank in front of each sentence if S. selects the correct number of coins *and* if S. says a word in the sentence for each coin.

Note: Say the sentences at a normal speaking rate. Do not emphasize the break between words. But be careful not to slur words together so that *Bill and I* becomes *Bill'n'I* or to stretch words out unnaturally so that *yesterday* becomes *yester-day*.

_____ 1. John smiled. (2 words)
_____ 2. She went shopping yesterday. (4 words)
_____ 3. Bill and I were playing cards. (6 words)

Total Correct: _____/3   Mastery Level: 3/3

1-B. Initial Consonants

(Teacher's page 3, no student page)

This time, you will need just two coins.

> T: Words are made up of individual sounds. Listen for the *first* sound you hear in each word. And listen for the *group* of sounds which make up the rest of the word.

> T: For example, if I say the word *cat*, the first sound in *cat* is /c/. (Select one coin for /c/, and place it in front of S.) And the rest of the sounds in *cat* are /at/. (Select one coin for /at/, and place it in front of S.)

Point to the coin on the left and say /c/. Point to the next coin and say /at/. Then blend /c/ and /at/ and say *cat*.

> T: (Point to the coin on the left.) What sound does this coin stand for? [S: /c/.] Yes, /c/. (Point to the next coin.) What sound does this coin stand for? [S:/at/.] Yes, /at/.

> T: I'm going to say some words. I want you to listen to the words. Then place a coin in front of you to show the sound you hear at the *beginning* of the word and say that sound. Place another coin to show the group of sounds you hear at the *end* of the word, and say that.

Say the words below. (The correct student responses are in parentheses.)

On teacher's scoring page 3, put a check in the blank if S. can separate the initial consonant from the rest of the word. S. should place one coin for the initial consonant and say it, then place another coin for the rest of the word and say it.

Do not count an item correct if S. is not able to separate the *initial* consonant from the spoken word. For example, *pet* and *pe-t* are both incorrect.

_____	1. pet	(p-et)
_____	2. cold	(c-old)
_____	3. sit	(s-it)
_____	4. made	(m-ade)
_____	5. loop	(l-oop)

Total Correct: _____/5   Mastery Level: 5/5

1-C. Final Consonants
(Teacher's page 3, no student page)

Again, you will need two coins.

> T: This time, I want you to listen for the *last* sound you hear in each word I say. You are going to use one coin for all the sounds that come before the last sound. Use another coin for the last sound.

> T: Let's try a word. If I say the word *pan*, the first group of sounds is /pa/. (Pronounce *pa* as in *pan*. As you say /pa/, place a coin in front of S.) And the last sound in *pan* is /n/. (As you say /n/, place one coin to the right of the first coin.)

> T: (Point to the coin on the left.) /pa/ (Point to the other coin.) /n/ (Sweep your finger across both coins.) *Pan.*

> T: (Point to the coin on the left.) What sound does this coin stand for? [S: /pa/.] Yes, /pa/. (Point to the other coin.) What sound does this coin stand for? [S:/n/.] Yes, /n/.

> T: I'm going to say some words. Listen to the words carefully. Place one coin in front of you to show the sounds you hear at the beginning of the word, and say those sounds. Then place another coin to show the sound at the end of the word, and say that sound.

Say the words below. (The correct student responses are in parentheses.)

On teacher's scoring page 3, put a check mark in the blank if S. can separate the final consonant from the rest of the word. S. should place one coin for the first group of sounds and say it, then place another coin for the final consonant and say it.

Do not count an item correct if S. is not able to separate the *final* consonant from the spoken word. For example, *pan* and *p-an* are both incorrect. Also, producing one coin and saying /n/ is incorrect.

_____	1. sun	(su-n)
_____	2. bad	(ba-d)
_____	3. hat	(ha-t)
_____	4. mop	(mo-p)
_____	5. leg	(le-g)

Total Correct: _____/5   Mastery Level: 5/5

2. AUDITORY DISCRIMINATION

2-A. Initial Consonants
(Teacher's page 4, no student page)

> T: I'm going to say a word. Listen carefully to the *beginning* sound in that word. Then I'm going to say two more words. You tell me which of the two words begins like my word.

> T: Let's try an example first. My word is *feather*. The other two words are *farmer* and *girl*. Which word starts like *feather*? [S: farmer.] Yes, *farmer* begins with the same sound as *feather*.

Say the words below. As S. answers, check his *correct* answers on teacher's page 4 of the reading profile booklet. If it becomes clear that S. is quite unable to do this task, stop and go on to 2-B.

_____ 1. dog	(ditch, farm)		_____ 10. little	(man, laugh)
_____ 2. mother	(hand, mask)		_____ 11. toast	(think, test)
_____ 3. cough	(couch, hope)		_____ 12. sun	(mean, soup)
_____ 4. jump	(jelly, fire)		_____ 13. number	(next, vine)
_____ 5. yellow	(weather, yeast)		_____ 14. zebra	(zoo, lady)
_____ 6. ghost	(sense, get)		_____ 15. fence	(last, fight)
_____ 7. wire	(fence, west)		_____ 16. parrot	(book, pig)
_____ 8. hope	(hollow, fire)		_____ 17. rose	(river, next)
_____ 9. baby	(basket, vest)		_____ 18. vest	(house, vine)

Total Correct: _____/ 18   Mastery Level: 16/ 18

2-B. Final Consonants
(Teacher's page 4, no student page)

> T: I'm going to say a word. Listen carefully to the *last* sound in that word. Then I will say two more words. You tell me which of the two words ends like my word.

> T: Here's an example. My word is *hat*. The other two words are *door* and *fit*. Which word ends like *hat*? [S: fit.] Yes, *fit* ends like *hat*.

Say the words below. As S. answers, check his *correct* answers on teacher's page 4 of the reading profile booklet. If it becomes clear that S. is quite unable to do this task, stop and go on to Part 3.

_____ 1. cab	(robe, sash)		_____ 7. road	(mud, girl)
_____ 2. hog	(raft, big)		_____ 8. like	(pick, tent)
_____ 3. man	(laugh, pin)		_____ 9. lime	(egg, seem)
_____ 4. stop	(sweep, tear)		_____ 10. core	(tear, moon)
_____ 5. leave	(save, more)		_____ 11. dress	(home, base)
_____ 6. call	(sun, full)		_____ 12. haze	(mean, doze)

Total Correct: _____/ 12   Mastery Level: 10/ 12

3. SOUNDS AND LETTERS

Give S. the Student Reading Profile with the student's pages remaining in it. Since you have removed the teacher's pages, student's page 7—where this section begins—will be the first page showing.

3-A. Names of Letters
(Teacher's page 5, student's page 7)

> T: Look at these letters. I'm going to point to them one by one. When I point to a letter, tell me if it is a capital or small letter, and tell me its *name*. The name of a letter is the way the letter is said when you say the alphabet.
>
> T: (Point to *E* on the student's page.) Here's an example. The name of this first letter is *capital E*. Now let's continue. I'll be checking off the ones you get correct.

Point to each letter on the student's page, going down each column. As S. answers, use teacher's page 5 to record *all* of the student's answers, as follows:

— Put a check in the blank if S. names the letter correctly. (Count the capital *E* as correct.)
— Leave blank if S. gives no answer.
— Write in the student's answer if he gives the wrong letter name. The teacher will then be able to analyze the kinds of errors the student makes.

Stop if S. misses any five items in a row. Then go on to 3-B.

___ E	___ i	___ W	___ B	___ h	___ I
___ P	___ S	___ n	___ v	___ A	___ m
___ K	___ T	___ r	___ g	___ U	___ L
___ l	___ o	___ e	___ z	___ D	___ C
___ M	___ Q	___ f	___ x	___ R	___ q
___ N	___ j	___ b	___ a	___ G	___ Y
___ d	___ H	___ F			

Total Correct: ___/39   Mastery Level: 37/39

3-B. Sounds for Letters

(Teacher's page 5, student's page 7)

> T: Now look at these letters. When I point to a letter, tell me the
> sound that the letter stands for. For example, the sound for the
> first letter is /e/. (Say the short *e* sound.) Now let's continue.

Point to each letter on the student's page, going down each column. For the last
column (*qu, ch, th, sh*), ask: "What sound do these two letters together stand for?" As
S. answers, use teacher's page 5 to record *all* of the student's answers, as follows:

— Put a check in the blank if S. gives the correct sound. (Count
the capital *E* as correct.)

— Leave blank if S. gives no answer.

— Write in the student's answer if he gives the wrong sound. The
teacher will then be able to analyze the kinds of errors the
student makes.

Stop if S. misses any five items in a row. Then go on to Part 4.

Note: If S. gives the long sound for a vowel, ask: "What is another sound for that
letter?" For *th,* accept either the sound in *thank* or the sound in *this.*

____ E	____ w	____ n	____ v	____ d	____ qu
____ k	____ H	____ s	____ x	____ R	____ ch
____ t	____ o	____ f	____ L	____ G	____ th
____ M	____ j	____ B	____ A	____ c	____ sh
____ P	____ i	____ z	____ u	____ y	

Total Correct: ____/29   Mastery Level: 25/29

4. WORD RECOGNITION
(Teacher's page 6, student's page 8)

> T: Read these words. If you don't know a word, say what you think it might be. If you still can't get it, say, "I don't know," and go on.

On teacher's page 6, record *all* of the student's answers, as follows:

— Put a check in the blank if S. reads the word correctly.
— Leave blank if S. gives no answer.
— Write in the student's answer if he gives the wrong word. The teacher will then be able to analyze the kinds of errors the student makes.

Stop if S. misses eight words in a row. Then go on to Part 5.

Note: If S. hesitates, after about five seconds, you may say the word and count it incorrect. If S. makes a mistake but then self-corrects it, the item should be counted correct.

_____	1. this	_____	13. he	_____	25. tell
_____	2. is	_____	14. not	_____	26. run
_____	3. the	_____	15. are	_____	27. shop
_____	4. to	_____	16. up	_____	28. thanks
_____	5. has	_____	17. says	_____	29. fish
_____	6. her	_____	18. do	_____	30. box
_____	7. she	_____	19. no	_____	31. name
_____	8. in	_____	20. looking	_____	32. street
_____	9. him	_____	21. puts	_____	33. Mr.
_____	10. and	_____	22. get	_____	34. Mrs.
_____	11. for	_____	23. one	_____	35. you
_____	12. at	_____	24. two	_____	36. give

Total Correct: _____/36   Mastery Level: 32/36

5. WRITING
(Teacher's page 6, student's page 8)

> T: (Point to the two sets of guidelines.) A name is printed on the first set of guidelines as an example for you. On the second set of guidelines, please print your name the way the example is printed.

Score the student's writing of his name as follows:

2 points: Letters are reasonably recognizable and well-formed.
1 point: Capital and lowercase letters are used correctly.
1 point: Space is left between words.

Total Correct: _____/4   Mastery Level: 3/4

6. PARTS OF WRITTEN LANGUAGE

6-A. Identifying Sentences
(Teacher's page 6, student's page 9)

> T: (Point to story 1.) Look over this story. How many sentences
> are in the story? Tell me the number of sentences.

S. may simply scan the story to determine the number of sentences. If he reads the complete story—either out loud or silently—do not stop him.

Repeat the process for story 2.

On teacher's page 6, write the number in the blank only if S. gives the correct number as the answer. Do not give any points for an incorrect answer.

_____ 1. (2 points for 2 sentences)
_____ 2. (3 points for 3 sentences)

Total Correct: _____/5   Mastery Level: 5/5

6-B. Identifying Paragraphs
(Teacher's page 6, student's page 9)

> T: Look over this story. How many paragraphs are in the story?
> Tell me the number of paragraphs.

S. may simply scan the story to determine the number of paragraphs. If he reads the complete story—either out loud or silently—do not stop him.

On teacher's page 6, record the number 4 in the blank only if S. gives the correct answer, 4. Do not give any points for an incorrect answer.

Total Correct: _____/4   Mastery Level: 4/4

6-C. Capitalization

(Student's page 10)

>T: This page is about using capital letters. In each group, the same sentence is written three different ways. The words are the same, but capital letters are used in different places. One sentence in the group is right, and the other two sentences are wrong.

Have S. read aloud the three sentences in number 1 to observe that the words are the same, but capital letters are used in different places.

>T: Put a check mark in the blank by the sentence that has capital letters in the right places.

Let S. complete the rest of this page by himself.

You can score this page and the remainder of Student Reading Profile 1 after S. has finished all of it.

>Answers: 1. c
>2. b
>3. a
>4. b

>Total Correct: _____/4   Mastery Level: 3/4

6-D. Punctuation

(Student's page 10)

>T: This page is about using punctuation marks. (Point to the punctuation marks in the box at the top of the page.)

>T: These are the punctuation marks that this page deals with. (Point to each mark as you say its name.) Period, exclamation point, question mark, apostrophe, and quotation marks.

>T: In each group below, the same sentence is written three different ways. The words are the same, but the punctuation marks are different. One sentence in the group is right, and the other two sentences are wrong.

Have S. read aloud the three sentences in number 1 to observe that the words are the same, but that the punctuation at the end is different.

>T: Put a check mark in the blank by the sentence that has the correct punctuation marks.

Let S. complete the rest of this page by himself.

>Answers: 1. a   3. a
>2. c   4. b

>Total Correct: _____/4   Mastery Level: 3/4

7. COMPREHENSION
(Student's pages 12-14)

> T: (Indicate pages 12 and 13.) On these two pages are seven very short stories. Read each story, and then read the three sentences below it. Put a check mark by the sentence that has the same meaning as the story.

Note: If necessary to help S. understand what to do, work through the first item together with S. (count it as a "free" correct answer). Allow S. to read aloud or silently, as he wishes. Stop if this exercise is clearly too difficult for S.

> T: (Point to the last story, number 8, on page 14.) Now read this story and the questions after it. Put a check mark in front of either *Yes* or *No* as your answer to each question.

Answers: 1. b   5. c   8. A. b. No
          2. c   6. a   B. a. Yes
          3. a   7. a   C. a. Yes
          4. c

Total Correct: _____/ 10   Mastery Level 8/ 10

After S. has completed the Student Reading Profile, you can—in private—score those parts that you have not already scored. Check the correct items. Transfer the total score for all parts to Summary Record 1.

At this time, you can remove the perforated student pages from the reading profile booklet and staple them together with the teacher's pages. The Summary Record should be on top.

Note: See Part 3 of this manual for instructions on placement and Part 4 for teaching suggestions.

SUMMARY RECORD 1
for Student Reading Profile 1

Student's name _____

Date _____ Person administering _____

		Total Correct	Mastery Level	
1.	**Segmentation**			
	1-A. Number of Words in a Sentence	_____/3	3/3	
	1-B. Initial Consonants	_____/5	5/5	
	1-C. Final Consonants	_____/5	5/5	
2.	**Auditory Discrimination**			
	2-A. Initial Consonants	_____/18	16/18	
	2-B. Final Consonants	_____/12	10/12	
3.	**Sounds and Letters**			
	3-A. Names of Letters	_____/39	37/39	
	3-B. Sounds for Letters	_____/29	25/29	
4.	**Word Recognition**	_____/36	32/36	
5.	**Writing**	_____/4	3/4	
6.	**Parts of Written Language**			
	6-A. Identifying Sentences	_____/5	5/5	
	6-B. Identifying Paragraphs	_____/4	4/4	
	6-C. Capitalization	_____/4	3/4	
	6-D. Punctuation	_____/4	3/4	
7.	**Comprehension**	_____/10	8/10	
	TOTAL	_____/178	159/178	

Administering Student Reading Profile 2

Student Reading Profile 2 reflects the instructional tasks included in *Skill Book 2* of the Laubach Way to Reading series. The six parts in this Student Reading Profile are:

1. Segmentation
2. Blending
3. Word Recognition
4. Consonant Blends and Digraphs
5. Word Parts
6. Comprehension

All pages in the Student Reading Profile booklet are perforated. Before you begin, tear out the teacher's pages at the front. In this booklet, they are the first two sheets of paper (pages 1-4). These teacher's pages are marked with a black border at the top and bottom to help you identify them.

You will use the teacher's pages from the booklet for scoring the first sections of the reading profile while S. is answering questions. Teacher's page 2 is the Summary Record, which you will use at the end to record the student's total scores for all sections of the Student Reading Profile.

Before beginning, explain to S. that doing this Student Reading Profile should take an hour to an hour and a half. Be very warm and supportive throughout the process of giving this reading profile. If S. becomes overly frustrated by any section of the profile, stop and go on to the next section.

1. SEGMENTATION

Note: In section 1-A and in a number of sections in this Student Reading Profile, S. is given an example or two for practice. It may happen that S. will have difficulty producing a correct response for a particular practice item. If so, before beginning the regular items, take time to explain both the practice task and the correct response. If S. then *still* cannot perform the task, try one or two regular items. Move on to the next section if S. also misses these items.

1-A: Segmenting Vowels in Words
(Teacher's page 3, <u>no student page</u>)

You will <u>need two coins</u>, preferably of the same denomination, for this section. No other student material is needed. Place the two coins in front of S.

> T: I'm going to say some words to you. Listen carefully. Each word will have <u>two sounds.</u> For each sound, place one coin here. (Point to a place in front of S. away from the coins.) Then tell me the sound for each coin you have put down.

> T: For example, in the word *me,* I hear two sounds. I hear /m/. (Select one coin and place it in front of S.) And I hear /ē/. (Select another coin and place it beside the other coin; coins should be in the student's left-right order.) The word *me* has the sounds /m/ and /ē/. (Point to one coin as you say each sound.)

> T: Show the sounds in *me* by pointing to the coins. Show me the coin that stands for /m/. [S. points to first coin.] Show me the coin that stands for /ē/. [S. points to second coin.] That's right. This coin stands for /m/, and this coin stands for /ē/.

> T: Now you try one yourself. Listen for the two sounds in *Ed.* Say the sounds in *Ed.* Place a coin in front of you to stand for *each sound* in *Ed.* [S. does the task.] Once more, point to the coins, and say the sounds in *Ed.* [S. points and says sounds.] Very good. Those are the sounds in *Ed.*

> T: Now I'm going to say some more words that have two sounds. For each word I say, place one coin in front of you as you say *each sound* in the word.

Say the words below. S. should put down two coins for each word, as you have already told him there are two sounds. S. must say the sound which each coin stands for. On teacher's page 3, put a check mark in the blank in front of each word if S. puts down two coins *and* says the correct sound for each. (The correct sounds are in parentheses.)

Note: You may pronounce words again during the task if necessary.

_____ 1. no   (n-o)
_____ 2. up   (u-p)
_____ 3. at   (a-t)
_____ 4. if   (i-f)
_____ 5. egg   (e-gg)

Total Correct: _____/5   Mastery Level: 5/5

1-B: Segmenting Words into Sounds
(Teacher's page 3, no student page)

Place five coins in front of S. in a mass.

> T: I'm going to say some more words. This time there will be *more* sounds in each of the words. You must listen carefully so you can hear each of the sounds. Place one coin in front of you for each sound you hear in the words I say. Then point to each coin and say the sounds.

> T: Here's an example. In the word *Sam,* I hear /s/ (place one coin in front of S.), /a/ (place a second coin), and /m/ (place a third coin). The sounds in *Sam* are /s/—/a/—/m/. (Point to each coin as you repeat the sounds.)

> T: Now you try one yourself. Listen for the sounds in *camp*. Say the sounds in *camp*. Place a coin in front of you to stand for *each sound* in *camp*. [S. does the task.] Once more, point to the coins, and say the sounds in *camp*. [S. points and says sounds: /c/—/a/—/m/—/p/.] Very good. Those are the sounds in *camp*.

> T: Now I'm going to say some more words. For each word I say, place one coin in front of you as you say *each sound* in the word.

Say the words below. S. must select the correct number of coins to stand for the sounds in each word. For each coin, S. must say the correct sound. On teacher's page 3, put a check mark in the blank in front of each word if S. selects the correct number of coins *and* if S. says the correct sound for each.

Note: Count items 2-5 correct if S. preserves the consonant blend (e.g., *sl-o-t*) or separates the blend (e.g., *s-l-o-t*). It is not correct if the vowel is joined to a consonant (e.g., *c-ol-d*). The consonant blends here are *sl, dr, ld, str.*

_____	1. hat	3:	(h-a-t)
_____	2. slot	3 or 4:	(sl-o-t) or (s-l-o-t)
_____	3. drop	3 or 4:	(dr-o-p) or (d-r-o-p)
_____	4. cold	3 or 4:	(c-o-ld) or (c-o-l-d)
_____	5. stripe	3, 4, or 5:	(str-i-pe) or (st-r-i-pe) or (s-t-r-i-pe)

Total Correct: _____/5   Mastery Level: 5/5

2. BLENDING
(Teacher's page 4, student's page 5)

Give S. the Student Reading Profile with the student's pages remaining in it. Since you have removed the teacher's pages, student's page 5—where this section begins—will be the first page showing.

> T: (Point to the nonsense words on the student's page.) The words in this part are nonsense words. Don't try to make them real words. Read the example. (Point to *fap*.)

If necessary, help S. by sounding out /f/—/a/—/p/ and then blending the sounds together to make *fap*. Then have S. read the other words by himself.

If S. reads the nonsense word correctly with a short vowel sound, count the item as correct. Put a check mark in the blank on teacher's page 4.

_____ 1. sud   _____ 3. rin   _____ 5. tef
_____ 2. mag   _____ 4. pom

Total Correct: _____/5   Mastery Level: 5/5

3. WORD RECOGNITION
(Teacher's page 4, student's page 5)

> T: Now read these <u>real words</u>. If you don't know a word, try to sound it out. If you still can't get it, say, "I don't know," and go on.

On teacher's page 4, record *all* of the student's answers, as follows:
— Put a check in the blank if S. reads the word correctly.
— Leave blank if S. gives no answer.
— Write in the student's answer if he gives the wrong word. This will help the teacher analyze the student's errors.

Stop if S. misses eight words in a row. Then go on to Part 4.

Note: If S. hesitates, after about five seconds, you may say the word and count it incorrect. If S. makes a mistake but then self-corrects it, the item should be counted correct.

_____ 1. work	_____ 16. them	_____ 31. many
_____ 2. after	_____ 17. were	_____ 32. let's
_____ 3. will	_____ 18. what	_____ 33. truck
_____ 4. picked	_____ 19. said	_____ 34. burn
_____ 5. friends	_____ 20. glass	_____ 35. fix
_____ 6. car	_____ 21. was	_____ 36. first
_____ 7. us	_____ 22. help	_____ 37. family
_____ 8. another	_____ 23. cannot	_____ 38. marry
_____ 9. stopped	_____ 24. that	_____ 39. sister
_____ 10. quick	_____ 25. comes	_____ 40. who
_____ 11. large	_____ 26. their	_____ 41. plan
_____ 12. from	_____ 27. cents	_____ 42. which
_____ 13. job	_____ 28. laugh	_____ 43. with
_____ 14. funny	_____ 29. dollar	_____ 44. bringing
_____ 15. hurried	_____ 30. little	_____ 45. son

Total Correct: _____/45   Mastery Level: 40/45

4. CONSONANT BLENDS AND DIGRAPHS

4-A. Initial Consonant Blends and Digraphs
(Student's page 6)

> T: I'm going to say some words. Listen for the *beginning* sounds. Circle the letters that my word starts with. (Point to the example line on the student's page.)

> T: Here's an example. My word is *twelve*. What are the beginning letters of *twelve?* Circle them. [S. circles *tw.*]

Say the words below. Score this section and the rest of the reading profile later.

(black)	1.	bl	br	dr
(grass)	2.	gl	gr	pr
(skirt)	3.	st	sl	sk
(pretty)	4.	pl	pr	tr
(when)	5.	wh	tw	fr
(stop)	6.	pr	tr	st
(clock)	7.	gl	cl	sk
(drop)	8.	tr	br	dr
(then)	9.	th	tw	wh
(friend)	10.	tr	fr	dr

Total Correct: _____ / 10   Mastery Level: 9/10

4-B. Final Consonant Blends and Digraphs
(Student's page 6)

> T: I'm going to say some more words. This time, listen for the *ending* sounds. Circle the letters that my word ends with. (Point to the example line on the student's page.)

> T: Here's an example. My word is *ranch*. What are the last letters of *ranch?* Circle them. [S. circles *nch.*]

Say the words below. Score this section later.

(bank)	1.	nt	nk	nd
(left)	2.	ft	st	th
(hand)	3.	nt	nk	nd
(sing)	4.	nch	nt	ng
(fast)	5.	sh	st	sk
(bath)	6.	th	sh	ft
(lunch)	7.	ng	nch	nk
(wish)	8.	th	st	sh

Total Correct: _____ /8   Mastery Level: 7/8

5. WORD PARTS

5-A. Endings
(Student's page 7)

> T: (Point to the words in the student's booklet.) Look at these words. I'm going to ask you to change each word by adding an ending. For example, this word is *hunt* (point to *hunt* at the top of the page). On the second set of guidelines, *hunt* is changed to *hunter*.

Say the words below, using this format:

> T: This word is ____. (Point to the printed word on the student's page.) Write the word ____. (Say the word with its ending.)

You may give an example sentence for each word with an ending, as needed. Stop if S. misses four items in a row. Then go on to 5-B.

2 pronunciations →

1. look	(looking)		6. help	(helped)
2. match	(matches)		7. get	(getting)
3. live	(lived)		8. give	(giving)
4. farm	(farmer)		9. yell	(yelled)
5. plan	(planned)		10. large	(larger)

Total Correct: ____/ 10   Mastery Level: 9/ 10

5-B. Substituting Beginning Consonant Sounds
(Student's page 8)

> T: (Point to the words on the student's page.) Look at these words. I'm going to ask you to make new words by changing the beginning sounds. For example, this word is *luck*. (Point to first example word.) Here, it is changed to *truck*. (Point to second example word.)

Say the words below, following this format:

> T: This word is ____. (Point to the word in the student's booklet.) Change the word to ____.

Stop if S. misses four items in a row. Then go on to Part 5-C.

1. sell	(tell)		6. hen	(when)
2. turn	(burn)		7. art	(part)
3. mop	(chop)		8. tank	(thank)
4. dish	(wish)		9. top	(stop)
5. back	(black)		10. ten	(then)

Total Correct: ____/ 10   Mastery Level: 9/ 10

5-C. Substituting Vowels
(Student's page 9)

> T: (Point to the words on the student's page.) Look at these words.
> Again, I'm going to ask you to make new words by changing
> part of the word. This time, you will change the *vowel*.
> Remember, the vowels are *a, e, i, o, u.*

> T: For example, this word is *nut.* (Point to first example word.)
> Here, we have changed *nut* to *net* by changing the vowel *u* to *e.*
> (Point to second example word.)

Say the words below, following this format:

> T: This word is _____ . (Point to the word in the student's booklet.)
> Change the word to _____ .

Stop if S. misses three items in a row. Then go on to Part 6.

1. pack	(pick)	4. fan	(fun)
2. ship	(shop)	5. stop	(step)
3. hot	(hat)		

Total Correct: _____/5   Mastery Level: 4/5

6. COMPREHENSION
(Student's pages 10-12)

Ask S. to read the stories and put a check mark next to the best answer. S. may read
silently or aloud. Stop if this exercise is clearly too difficult for S.

Answers:	1. a	3. c	5. A. c	6. A. b	7. A. a
	2. b	4. b	B. b	B. c	B. b

Total Correct: _____/10   Mastery Level: 8/10

After S. has completed the Student Reading Profile, you can—in private—score
those parts that you have not already scored. Check the correct items. Transfer the
total score for all parts to Summary Record 2.

At this time, you can remove the perforated student pages from the reading profile
booklet and staple them together with the teacher's pages. The Summary Record
should be on top.

Note: See Part 3 of this manual for instructions on placement and Part 4 for teaching
suggestions.

SUMMARY RECORD 2
for Student Reading Profile 2

Student's name _____

Date _____ Person administering _____

		Total Correct	Mastery Level
1.	**Segmentation**		
	1-A. Segmenting Vowels in Words	_____/5	5/5
	1-B. Segmenting Words into Sounds	_____/5	5/5
2.	**Blending**	_____/5	5/5
3.	**Word Recognition**	_____/45	40/45
4.	**Consonant Blends and Digraphs**		
	4-A. Initial Consonant Blends and Digraphs	_____/10	9/10
	4-B. Final Consonant Blends and Digraphs	_____/8	7/8
5.	**Word Parts**		
	5-A. Endings	_____/10	9/10
	5-B. Substituting Beginning Consonant Sounds	_____/10	9/10
	5-C. Substituting Vowels	_____/5	4/5
6.	**Comprehension**	_____/10	8/10
	TOTAL	_____/113	101/113

Administering Student Reading Profile 3

Student Reading Profile 3 reflects the instructional tasks included in *Skill Book 3* of the Laubach Way to Reading series. The five parts in this Student Reading Profile are:

1. Word Recognition
2. Word Parts
3. Spelling
4. Comprehension
5. Practical Reading and Writing

All pages in the Student Reading Profile booklet are perforated. Before you begin, tear out the teacher's pages at the front. In this booklet, they are the first two sheets of paper (pages 1-4). These teacher's pages are marked with a black border at the top and bottom to help you identify them.

You will use the teacher's pages from the booklet for scoring the first section of the reading profile while S. is answering questions. Teacher's page 2 is the Summary Record, which you will use at the end to record the student's total scores for all sections of the Student Reading Profile.

Before beginning, explain to S. that doing this Student Reading Profile should take an hour to an hour and a half. Be very warm and supportive throughout the process of giving this reading profile. If S. becomes overly frustrated by any section of the profile, stop and go on to the next section.

1. WORD RECOGNITION
(Teacher's page 3, student's page 5)

Give S. the Student Reading Profile with the student's pages remaining in it. Since you have removed the teacher's pages, student's page 5—where this section begins—will be the first page showing.

> T: We are going to start by having you read some words. Read each word aloud. If you aren't sure of a word, try to sound it out or say what you think it might be. If you still can't get it, say, "I don't know," and go on.

On teacher's page 3, record *all* of the student's answers, as follows:
— Put a check in the blank if S. reads the word correctly.
— Leave blank if S. gives no answer.
— Write in the student's answer if he gives the wrong word. The teacher will then be able to analyze the kinds of errors the student makes.

Stop if S. misses seven words in a row. Then go on to Part 2.

Note: If S. hesitates, after about five seconds, you may say the word and count it incorrect. If S. makes a mistake but then self-corrects it, the item should be counted correct.

_____ 1. alone	_____ 17. here	_____ 33. spoken
_____ 2. paid	_____ 18. homework	_____ 34. write
_____ 3. nice	_____ 19. license	_____ 35. sleepy
_____ 4. bake	_____ 20. loaf	_____ 36. table
_____ 5. beans	_____ 21. cities	_____ 37. stairs
_____ 6. night	_____ 22. forty	_____ 38. teeth
_____ 7. away	_____ 23. where	_____ 39. I'll
_____ 8. dear	_____ 24. money	_____ 40. these
_____ 9. corner	_____ 25. won't	_____ 41. snow
_____ 10. cry	_____ 26. music	_____ 42. united
_____ 11. die	_____ 27. cheaper	_____ 43. oldest
_____ 12. care	_____ 28. radio	_____ 44. tried
_____ 13. wild	_____ 29. retired	_____ 45. most
_____ 14. before	_____ 30. want	_____ 46. find
_____ 15. flight	_____ 31. Friday	_____ 47. thirty-three
_____ 16. safely	_____ 32. eighteen	_____ 48. there

Total Correct: _____/48   Mastery Level: 43/48

2. WORD PARTS

2-A. Compound Words
(Student's page 5)

Introduce this section and read the directions on the student's page to the student as shown below.

> T: This part is about words that have two smaller words in them. Read the big word. Then write the two short words that you see in it. Here's an example. (Point to example on student's page.) The big word is *homework*. The two short words in it are *home* and *work*.

Let S. complete this section by himself. Score this section and all remaining parts of the Student Reading Profile after S. has finished all of it.

Answers:	1. week end	4. pay check
	2. land lady	5. some times
	3. any one	6. my self

Total Correct: _____/6   Mastery Level: 6/6

2-B. Contractions
(Student's page 6)

> T: In this part, you will read the word. Then write the two words that it comes from. The example word is *it's*. The two words that it comes from are *it* and *is*.

Let S. complete this section by himself. When scoring, count the answer as correct only if it is spelled correctly.

Answers:		
	1. I am	4. we will
	2. was not	5. you are
	3. what is	6. do not

Total Correct: _____/6   Mastery Level: 5/6

2-C. Endings
(Student's page 6)

> T: (Point to the words in the student's booklet.) Look at these words. I'm going to ask you to change each word by adding an ending. For example, this word is *party*. (Point to example.) It is changed to *parties*. (Point.)

Say the words below, using this format:

> T: This word is _____. (Point to the printed word on the student's page.) Write the word _____. (Say the word with its ending.)

You may give an example sentence for each word with an ending, as needed.

1. high	(higher)	5. slow	(slowly)
2. sun	(sunny)	6. nice	(nicer)
3. fast	(fastest)	7. big	(biggest)
4. cry	(cries)	8. carry	(carried)

Total Correct: _____/8   Mastery Level: 7/8

3. SPELLING
(Student's page 6)

> T: Now you will do some spelling. There are 20 spelling words. Listen carefully as I say each word. Then listen, and I will give you a sentence with the word in it. After that, write the word in the space. Even if you aren't sure of the spelling, give each word a try.

Give the number, then the word, then the example sentence. You may repeat the word and example if necessary.

1. take	Please *take* the food home.
2. coat	She was wearing a red *coat*.
3. tie	He forgot to *tie* his shoes.
4. meal	That was a good *meal*.
5. paint	I want to *paint* my kitchen.
6. near	We live *near* the school.
7. window	The *window* was open.
8. dry	It was wet, but now it's *dry*.
9. play	The puppy wants to *play*.
10. wheel	A car has a steering *wheel*.
11. tore	I *tore* my new shirt.
12. smile	He has a nice *smile*.
13. valley	They live in a *valley*.
14. share	Will you *share* your lunch with me?
15. tired	She felt *tired*.
16. morning	I had breakfast this *morning*.
17. right	Make a *right* turn here.
18. chair	Please sit on that *chair*.
19. evening	We watched TV yesterday *evening*.
20. woke	She *woke* up early this morning.

Total Correct: _____/20   Mastery Level: 17/20

4. COMPREHENSION
(Student's pages 7-8)

4-A. Three Days at Snake River

T: In Part 4, you will read a story and then answer questions about the story. Then you will do the same with a second story.

T: (Point to the story on page 7.) This story is about the Masons' trip. You may read the story silently or aloud, as you prefer. Then answer the questions about it. As you answer the questions, you can look back at the story.

In the answers, spelling does not count, and the sentence need not be grammatically correct or grammatically complete.

Answers to 4-A:
1. b. to Snake River.
2. Any sentence about having fun, fishing, playing in the water, or picking up pretty rocks.
3. a. Yes.
4. A hundred dollars (may be written $100).

4-B. Fire at Home

> T: This story is about a fire at Joe's house. Read the story, and then follow the directions below it.

Note: If S. has difficulty understanding the instructions on page 8, offer help. To make the task on page 8 easier, you may print each of the six sentences on a separate slip of paper. Then have S. place the slips of paper in the proper order.

Answers to 4-B:
2. Joe went to sleep.
1. Joe was smoking in bed.
6. The fire was put out.
4. The puppy woke Joe up.
3. The bed started burning.
5. Joe called the fire department.

Total Correct for Part 4: ____ / 10   Mastery Level: 8/ 10

5. PRACTICAL READING AND WRITING
(Student's pages 9-12)

> T: This section is about the kind of practical reading and writing a person does in everyday life. On each page, there are instructions which we will read together. Then there is something for you to read. And then there are some questions for you to answer.

> T: Now read the directions at the top of page 9. I'll help you with difficult words. Then, follow the directions.

Watch to see that S. understands what to do. If S. gets confused, explain again what to do. When S. finishes page 9, have S. continue with pages 10 through 12. Help S. with any difficult words in the directions. For the application on page 12, be sure S. understands that he is to fill in the form about himself.

If S. becomes overly frustrated by any of these tasks, encourage him to move on to the next section. Try not to end Part 5 until S. has attempted all the tasks.

Answers to Part 5:

5-A. Check
1. Kay Block
2. Helen Porter
3. April 30, 1995
4. May rent
5. $375.00 (may be spelled out)

Total Correct: _____/5
Mastery Level: 5/5

5-B. Letter
1. Carla
2. Gail and Jason
3. April 3, 1995
4. b
5. May 28 (1995 is optional)
6. 2:00 p.m. Pages 59–60

Total Correct: _____/6
Mastery Level: 6/6

5-C. Bill
1. Brake repair
2. Labor
3. $2.50
4. $38.00

Total Correct: _____/4
Mastery Level: 4/4

5-D. Timetable
1. 8:55 a.m.
2. 1:20 p.m.
3. (Gate) 3
4. 505 and 675
5. 9:25 a.m.

Total Correct: _____/5
Mastery Level: 4/5

5-E. Application
Score 1 point for each of the following items. Answers must be spelled correctly. Appropriate abbreviations are acceptable, as is a number for the month.

1 — Last Name	Address:	Date of Birth:	1 — Age
1 — First Name	1 — Number and Street	1 — Month	1 — Sex
	1 — City	1 — Day	1 — Signature
	1 — State	1 — Year	
	1 — Zip Code		

Total Correct: _____/12
Mastery Level: 11/12

After S. has completed the Student Reading Profile, you can—in private—score those parts that you have not already scored. Check the correct items. Transfer the total score for all parts to Summary Record 3.

At this time, you can remove the perforated student pages from the reading profile booklet and staple them together with the teacher's pages. The Summary Record should be on top.

Note: See Part 3 of this manual for instructions on placement and Part 4 for teaching suggestions.

SUMMARY RECORD 3
for Student Reading Profile 3

Student's name _____

Date _____ Person administering _____

	Total Correct	Mastery Level
1. Word Recognition	_____ /48	43/48
2. Word Parts		
2-A. Compound Words	_____ /6	6/6
2-B. Contractions	_____ /6	5/6
2-C. Endings	_____ /8	7/8
3. Spelling	_____ /20	17/20
4. Comprehension	_____ /10	8/10
5. Practical Reading and Writing		
5-A. Check	_____ /5	5/5
5-B. Letter	_____ /6	6/6
5-C. Bill	_____ /4	4/4
5-D. Timetable	_____ /5	4/5
5-E. Application	_____ /12	11/12
TOTAL	_____ /130	116/130

Administering Student Reading Profile 4

Student Reading Profile 4 reflects the instructional tasks included in *Skill Book 4* of the Laubach Way to Reading series. The six parts in this Student Reading Profile are:

1. Word Recognition
2. Word Parts
3. Word Meanings
4. Comprehension
5. Spelling
6. Practical Reading

All pages in the Student Reading Profile booklet are perforated. Before you begin, tear out the teacher's pages at the front. In this booklet, they are the first two sheets of paper (pages 1-4). These teacher's pages are marked with a black border at the top and bottom to help you identify them.

You will use the teacher's pages from the booklet for scoring the first sections of the reading profile while S. is answering questions. Teacher's page 2 is the Summary Record, which you will use at the end to record the student's total scores for all sections of the Student Reading Profile.

Before beginning, explain to S. that doing this Student Reading Profile should take an hour to an hour and a half. Be very warm and supportive throughout the process of giving this reading profile. If S. becomes overly frustrated by any section of the profile, stop and go on to the next section.

1. WORD RECOGNITION
(Teacher's page 3, student's page 5)

Give S. the Student Reading Profile with the student's pages remaining in it. Since you have removed the teacher's pages, student's page 5—where this section begins—will be the first page showing.

> T: Please read these words. If you don't know a word, try to sound it out. If you still can't get it, say, "I don't know," and go on.

On teacher's page 3, record *all* of the student's answers, as follows:

— Put a check in the blank if S. reads the word correctly.
— Leave blank if S. gives no answer.
— Write in the student's answer if he gives the wrong word. The teacher will then be able to analyze the kinds of errors the student makes.

Stop if S. misses seven words in a row. Then go on to Part 2.

Note: If S. hesitates, after about five seconds, you may say the word and count it incorrect. If S. makes a mistake but then self-corrects it, the item should be counted correct.

_____ 1. crawl	_____ 21. national	_____ 41. hour
_____ 2. cure	_____ 22. climb	_____ 42. January
_____ 3. pull	_____ 23. machine	_____ 43. discussion
_____ 4. should	_____ 24. Tuesday	_____ 44. although
_____ 5. almost	_____ 25. fault	_____ 45. poor
_____ 6. wrap	_____ 26. true	_____ 46. beautiful
_____ 7. about	_____ 27. mechanic	_____ 47. square
_____ 8. daughter	_____ 28. insurance	_____ 48. through
_____ 9. experience	_____ 29. tough	_____ 49. avoid
_____ 10. cough	_____ 30. choose	_____ 50. couldn't
_____ 11. pleasure	_____ 31. amusement	_____ 51. thought
_____ 12. weigh	_____ 32. knock	_____ 52. energy
_____ 13. review	_____ 33. caught	_____ 53. small
_____ 14. decision	_____ 34. accept	_____ 54. June
_____ 15. rescue	_____ 35. emergency	_____ 55. newspaper
_____ 16. occupation	_____ 36. rough	_____ 56. pleasant
_____ 17. physical	_____ 37. schedule	_____ 57. shook
_____ 18. usually	_____ 38. employee	_____ 58. August
_____ 19. crowd	_____ 39. headache	_____ 59. annoy
_____ 20. useless	_____ 40. bought	_____ 60. shoot

Total Correct: _____/60   Mastery Level: 54/60

2. WORD PARTS

T: The next three sections are about parts of words. In each section, there are instructions and an example for you to follow.

2-A. Contractions

(Student's page 5)

Have S. read the directions for 2-A. Help him with any difficult words. Then go over the example with him. As S. begins, watch to see that he understands what to do. If S. gets confused, explain again what to do.

This part and the remainder of the Student Reading Profile may be scored after S. has finished all of it.

Answers: 1. I'm   4. they'll
           2. we're   5. wouldn't
           3. haven't   6. here's

Total Correct: _____/6   Mastery Level: 6/6

2-B. Compound Words
(Student's page 6)

Have S. read the directions for 2-B. Help him with any difficult words. Then go over the example with him. As S. begins, watch to see that he understands what to do. If S. gets confused, explain again what to do.

Answers: Answers may be in any order, not just this order.
1. Example—no score   6. grandchildren
2. baseball   7. overdose
3. bedroom   8. rowboat
4. bookkeeping   9. sidewalk
5. downtown   10. watchdog

Total Correct: _____/9   Mastery Level: 8/9

2-C. Suffixes
(Student's page 6)

Have S. read the directions for 2-C. Help him with any difficult words. Then go over the example with him. As S. begins, watch to see that he understands what to do. If S. gets confused, explain again what to do.

Answers: 1. Example—no score   6. -ful
2. -less   7. -or
3. -hood   8. -ship
4. -ment   9. -al
5. -ous   10. -ness

Total Correct: _____/9   Mastery Level: 8/9

3. WORD MEANINGS

T: The next two sections are about word meanings.

3-A. Words That Mean the Same
(Student's page 7)

Have S. read the directions. Help him with any difficult words. Then go over the example with him.

Answers: 1. Example—no score   7. physician: doctor
2. almost: nearly   8. recreation: fun
3. chef: cook   9. scream: shout
4. sad: unhappy   10. silent: quiet
5. improved: better   11. strange: unusual
6. nation: country   12. wrong: incorrect

Total Correct: _____/11   Mastery Level: 10/11

3-B. Words That Mean the Opposite
(Student's page 7)

Have S. read the directions. Help him with any difficult words. Then go over the example with him.

Answers:
1. Example—no score		7. famous
2. smooth		8. huge
3. rich		9. weak
4. peace		10. safety
5. full		11. enemy
6. strength		12. short

Total Correct: _____ / 11   Mastery Level: 10/11

4. COMPREHENSION
(Student's pages 8-9)

> T: In this part, you will read a story and then answer some questions about it. Then you will do the same for another story.
> As you answer the questions, you may look back at the story.

Allow S. to read silently or aloud, as he prefers. When S. has finished answering the questions for the first story, have him go on to the second one.

In the answers, spelling does not count, and the sentence need not be grammatically correct or grammatically complete.

Answers to 4-A:
1. The south side.
2. c
3. c
4. b
5. c

Answers to 4-B.
1. In the Senate Office Building.
2. b
3. A sentence should indicate that the day care center will stay open long hours because Senate employees must often work late.
4. b
5. c

Total Correct for Part 4: _____ / 10   Mastery Level: 8/10

5. SPELLING
(Student's page 10)

> T: Now you will do some spelling. There are 20 spelling words. Listen carefully as I say each word. Then listen, and I will give you a sentence with the word in it. After that, write the word in the space. Even if you aren't sure of a spelling, give each word a try.

Give the number, then the word, then the example sentence. You may repeat the word and example if necessary.

1.	used	I bought a *used* car.
2.	noise	That music sounds like *noise* to me.
3.	could	I wish I *could* sing.
4.	found	First he lost it, then he *found* it.
5.	action	It's time to take *action*.
6.	knew	I *knew* it was a mistake.
7.	wall	There is a high *wall* around that building.
8.	argue	Please don't *argue* with each other.
9.	frown	He had a *frown* on his face.
10.	January	The first month of the year is *January*.
11.	stood	After sitting a long time, we *stood* up.
12.	awful	An *awful* thing happened.
13.	happiness	Some people find *happiness* in their work.
14.	taught	My mother *taught* me to drive.
15.	school	He works at a market after *school*.
16.	cause	What was the *cause* of the accident?
17.	unemployed	She was *unemployed* for three months.
18.	thought	I *thought* I heard something.
19.	accident	In the *accident,* two cars crashed.
20.	although	He is very strong *although* he is small.

Total Correct: _____/20   Mastery Level: 17/20

6. PRACTICAL READING
(Student's pages 10-12)

> T: This section is about the kind of practical reading and writing a person does in everyday life. On each page, there are instructions which we will read together. Then there is something for you to read. And then there are some questions for you to answer.

> T: Now read the directions for 6-A on page 10. I'll help you with difficult words. Then, follow the directions.

Watch to see that S. understands what to do. If S. gets confused, explain again what to do. When S. finishes Part 6-A on page 10, have S. continue with pages 11 and 12. Help S. with any difficult words in the directions.

If S. becomes overly frustrated by any of these tasks, encourage him to move on to the next section. Try not to end Part 6 until S. has attempted all the tasks.

Answers to Part 6: **6-A. Want Ads**
1. 376 Circle Drive.
2. After 5:30.
3. The landlord.
4. Nurse's aide.
5. In person.
6. 2-5 p.m.

Total Correct: ____/6   Mastery Level: 5/6

6-B. Table of Contents
1. The Constitution
2. 65
3. a. Chapter 6
   b. 71
4. a. Chapter 3
   b. 40

Total Correct: ____/6   Mastery Level: 5/6

6-C. Dictionary

picnic — pig	damp — dark
piece	dance
picture	danger
pie	dare

1. b
2. a

Total Correct: ____/8   Mastery Level: 7/8

After S. has completed the Student Reading Profile, you can—in private—score those parts that you have not already scored. Check the correct items. Transfer the total score for all parts to Summary Record 4.

At this time, you can remove the perforated student pages from the reading profile booklet and staple them together with the teacher's pages. The Summary Record should be on top.

Note: See Part 3 of this manual for instructions on placement and Part 4 for teaching suggestions.

SUMMARY RECORD 4
for Student Reading Profile 4

Student's name _____

Date _____ Person administering _____

		Total Correct	Mastery Level
1.	**Word Recognition**	_____ /60	54/60
2.	**Word Parts**		
	2-A. Contractions	_____ /6	6/6
	2-B. Compound Words	_____ /9	8/9
	2-C. Suffixes	_____ /9	8/9
3.	**Word Meanings**		
	3-A. Words That Mean the Same	_____ /11	10/11
	3-B. Words That Mean the Opposite	_____ /11	10/11
4.	**Comprehension**	_____ /10	8/10
5.	**Spelling**	_____ /20	17/20
6.	**Practical Reading**		
	6-A. Want Ads	_____ /6	5/6
	6-B. Table of Contents	_____ /6	5/6
	6-C. Dictionary	_____ /8	7/8
	TOTAL	_____ /156	138/156

—— Part 3 ——
Placement

Placing the Student in the LWR Series

PLACEMENT OF THE STUDENT

After administering one of the Student Reading Profiles, consult the appropriate section below for instructions on placing the student.

After Scoring Student Reading Profile 1

Consult Summary Record 1 for the record of a student's areas of mastery and non-mastery.

You may start your student in *Skill Book 2* if:

      A. his or her total score was at mastery level,

         or

      B. his or her scores were at mastery level on these parts:

          1. Segmentation
          3. Sounds and Letters
          4. Word Recognition
          5. Writing
          7. Comprehension.

If the student scored at mastery level in all parts listed in B above, but his writing showed serious deficiencies in ability to form legible letters, use the Writing Lesson and Homework sections of the lessons in *Skill Book 1* before going on to *Skill Book 2*.

If your student's total score was near mastery level (in the 120-158 range), you may choose to begin with *Skill Book 1,* using the Alternative Method for Teaching Lessons 1-5 described in the *LWR Teacher's Manual for Skill Book 1,* pages 94-96. Otherwise, begin in *Skill Book 1,* following the regular method.

After Scoring Student Reading Profile 2

Consult Summary Record 2 for the record of a student's areas of mastery and non–mastery.

You may start your student in *Skill Book 3* if:

        A. his or her total score was at mastery level,

          or

        B. his or her scores were at mastery level on these parts:

          2. Blending

          3. Word Recognition

          5. Word Parts

          6. Comprehension.

Otherwise, begin the student in *Skill Book 2*. If the student did not achieve mastery in Blending (Part 2), however, you should do some work on this before beginning *Skill Book 2*. See the suggestions for blending in Part 4 of this manual.

Note: It is possible for a student to score well enough to begin in *Skill Book 3,* but not to score at mastery level on Segmentation (Part 1). If this is the case with your student, as you teach in *Skill Book 3,* look carefully for indications that the student may be memorizing but not truly learning the lessons. Students who have difficulty with the segmenting tasks might *seem* to have more reading skills than they actually do.

After Scoring Student Reading Profile 3

Consult Summary Record 3 for the record of a student's areas of mastery and non–mastery.

You may start your student in *Skill Book 4* if his or her total score was at mastery level.

If the student's scores were at mastery level in everything except Practical Reading and Writing (Part 5), go through the Reading for Living sections of the lessons in *Skill Book 3* before beginning *Skill Book 4*.

If the student's scores were at mastery level in everything except Spelling (Part 3), you may want to use books in the Focus on Phonics series—emphasizing spelling instead of reading—before beginning *Skill Book 4*. See suggestions on spelling in Part 4 of this manual.

Otherwise, begin the student in *Skill Book 3*.

After Scoring Student Reading Profile 4

Consult Summary Record 4 for the record of a student's areas of mastery and non-mastery.

If the student's total scores are at the mastery level, that suggests referral to a higher level set of materials—such as the appropriate level in the Challenger Adult Reading Series—or to a higher level program.

If the student's scores were at mastery level in everything except Practical Reading (Part 6), go through the Reading for Living sections of the lessons in Skill Book 4.

If the student's scores were at mastery level in everything except Spelling (Part 3), you may want to use books in the Focus on Phonics series—emphasizing spelling instead of reading. See suggestions on spelling in Part 4 of this manual.

Otherwise, begin the student in *Skill Book 4*.

PREPARATION FOR THE TUTOR

As you go through a skill book with the student, concentrate especially on areas in which he did not score at mastery level on the Student Reading Profile he took. Refer to Part 4 for further teaching suggestions for these skill areas.

It will also be helpful if the person administering the Student Reading Profile prepares for the tutor's use the Checklist of Skills to Emphasize, which appears on the following pages. (The Checklist is given here as a blackline master, from which you may make photocopies.)

The person filling out the Checklist should analyze the kinds of errors the student made in each section of non-mastery and add notes that will be useful to the tutor. For example, if the student needs work on adding endings to words, you might indicate which endings seem most troublesome. Or it might be that the student needs work on changing final *y* to *i* before various endings. If a student had difficulties with word recognition, you should indicate any observable patterns—such as particular spellings for a vowel sound, or beginning or ending consonant blends, or words with endings.

DIAGNOSTIC INVENTORY

Checklist of Skills to Emphasize

Student's name _____ Date _____

Person filling out checklist _____

1. Student may be placed in _____

2. Any preliminary work needed before beginning in materials named in #1.

_____

SKILL BOOK LEVEL	SKILL AREA (Check if not mastered.)	NOTES TO TUTOR
	Segmentation	
1	☐ Number of Words in a Sentence _____	
1	☐ Initial Consonants _____	
1	☐ Final Consonants _____	
2	☐ Segmenting Vowels in Words _____	
2	☐ Segmenting Words into Sounds _____	
	Sounds and Letters	
1	☐ Names of Letters _____	
1	☐ Sounds for Letters _____	
	Auditory Discrimination	
1	☐ Initial Consonants _____	
1	☐ Final Consonants _____	
2	☐ **Blending** _____	
	Consonant Blends and Digraphs	
2	☐ Initial Consonant Blends and Digraphs _____	
2	☐ Final Consonant Blends and Digraphs _____	

SKILL BOOK LEVEL	SKILL AREA (Check if not mastered.)	NOTES TO TUTOR

1-2-3-4 ☐ **Word Recognition** _____

_____

Parts of Written Language

1 ☐ Identifying Sentences _____

1 ☐ Identifying Paragraphs _____

1 ☐ Capitalization _____

1 ☐ Punctuation _____

Word Parts

2 ☐ Substituting Beginning Consonant Sounds _____

2 ☐ Substituting Vowels _____

2-3 ☐ Endings _____

3-4 ☐ Compound Words _____

3-4 ☐ Contractions _____

4 ☐ Suffixes _____

Word Meanings

4 ☐ Words That Mean the Same _____

4 ☐ Words That Mean the Opposite _____

1-2-3-4 ☐ **Comprehension** _____

3-4 ☐ **Practical Reading and Writing** _____

Writing

1 ☐ Manuscript (printing) _____

3 ☐ Cursive (handwriting) _____

3-4 ☐ **Spelling** _____

—— Part 4 ——
Using the Results in Teaching

Using the Results
of the LWR Diagnostic Inventory
in Teaching

As you go through a skill book with a student, concentrate especially on skill areas in which he or she did not score at mastery level in the Student Reading Profile that was given. Then, if you feel your student needs still more practice in a particular reading skill, return to this section for ideas on additional activities and materials.

Each skill book in the Laubach Way to Reading has an accompanying teacher's manual. At the beginning of each teacher's manual is a scope and sequence chart titled "Skills Introduced or Reinforced in Skill Book ____." Refer to this chart to find lessons in which there are exercises on a particular skill. The chart refers both to exercises that appear in the skill book itself and to those exercises described only in the teacher's manual which are to be done orally or on the blackboard with the student. Exercises that appear only in the teacher's manual are usually part of the Skills Practice section of each lesson. After finding the lessons in the scope and sequence chart, you can then refer to the table of contents in the teacher's manual for specific page references in both the skill book and the manual.

You may also find it helpful to refer to the two sections at the end of each lesson in the teacher's manual: Checking Progress and Meeting Individual Needs. There, you will find ideas for other reinforcement activities.

Additional supplementary materials referred to here include the Focus on Phonics series and the More Stories books. The Focus on Phonics series is designed to supplement skill books in the LWR series with additional practice on phonics and word analysis skills. A Focus on Phonics workbook may be used along with the LWR skill book of the same number. Practice numbers in a Focus on Phonics workbook correspond with lesson numbers in the LWR skill book of the same level.

For each level of the LWR series, there is a supplementary More Stories reader. In the reader, there are three additional reading selections for each lesson in the skill book. The vocabulary in the stories is controlled to the vocabulary taught in the skill books up to that point.

The following is a list of all of the skills covered in Student Reading Profiles 1-4, along with suggestions for teaching. The skill book level is indicated where appropriate.

SEGMENTATION: Level 1

In Student Reading Profile 1, the segmentation exercises assess a student's readiness for reading. If a student does not achieve mastery on the segmentation sections, do some readiness exercises of the type below before beginning *Skill Book 1* with your student.

Number of Words in a Sentence

- Say some short sentences which have only one–syllable words, such as:

  Look at the man.
  Walk to the store.
  Read the book.

  Ask S. to tap the table once for each word in a sentence. Tap along with S. if this is needed. Then have S. put down one coin for each word in a sentence.

- Choose some short sentences with one- and two-syllable words. This time, say a sentence, then pause after each word, allowing time for S. to put down a coin for each word. After the coins are placed, put them in a mass again. Then say each sentence at a normal speaking pace. After each sentence, have S. place one coin for each word, as he says each word.

Initial Consonants

- Choose some one-syllable words beginning with one consonant. Say a word to S., and have S. repeat. Then say the word, separating the initial consonant, and have S. repeat, placing one coin for the beginning consonant and one for the rest of the word. Then say a different word with the same initial consonant, and have S. try to separate the initial consonant, placing coins. For example:

T: let.
S: let.

T: l-et.
S: l-et.

T: lot.
S: l-ot.

- Print the words you used in the exercise above. Have S. circle the initial consonants, and have S. say the words, separating the initial consonants (e.g. *l-et, l-ot*).

Final Consonants

- Follow the methods for initial consonants, except this time separate the final consonant.

SEGMENTATION: Level 2

Segmenting Vowels in Words

Choose some one-syllable words which contain just two sounds (e.g., *go*). Say a word, and have S. repeat. Then say the word, separating the two sounds, and have S. repeat, placing one coin for each sound. Say the complete word now, and have S. try to separate the sounds, using the coins. For example:

T: go.
S: go.

T: /g/ — /ō/.
S: /g/ — /ō/.

T: go.
S: /g/ — /ō/.

Go over the same word several times this way if necessary. Print the word on paper. Have S. put a coin on the letter that stands for each sound as you say it.

Segmenting Words into Sounds

Using words with three or four sounds, follow the pattern demonstrated in this example:

T: plot.
S: plot.

T: Separate the sounds. Say: /pl/—/ot/.
S: /pl/—/ot/.

T: /pl/.
S: /pl/.

T: Separate the sounds in /pl/. Say: /p/—/l/.
S: /p/—/l/.

T: plot. Say: /ot/.
S: /ot/.

T: Separate the sounds in /ot/. Say: /o/—/t/.
S: /o/—/t/.

T: plot. Try to separate all the sounds.
Say: /p/—/l/—/o/—/t/.
S: /p/—/l/—/o/—/t/.

SOUNDS AND LETTERS: Level 1

Names of Letters

- If S. has difficulty with a letter, go back to the *Skill Book 1* lesson where it is first taught.

- Have S. copy a letter; then have S. name the letter. After S. copies and names a letter, have S. try to write the letter from memory.

- In *Focus on Phonics-1: Sounds and Names of Letters,* the part on Beginning Sounds and Letters contains naming exercises. The first two sections for each letter are particularly useful for naming. The last section is useful for visual discrimination of a letter from other letters with a similar shape.

- Make flash cards of the lowercase letters. Reteach each letter, eliminating cards that S. calls correctly at least four or five times when the card is presented. Have S. practice writing (printing) any of the letters that are particularly troublesome.

- If S. has difficulty relating the lowercase and capital forms of the same letter, use flash cards to have him match. Give only a few pairs at a time.

Sounds for Letters

- Use flash cards as for letter names, except have S. give the sounds instead.

- In *Focus on Phonics-1,* use the part on Beginning Sounds and Letters.

Sounds and Names of Letters

- Use the *Consonant Sounds and Letters Student Video* and exercises in the accompanying *Consonant Sounds and Letters Photocopy Masters.*

AUDITORY DISCRIMINATION: Level 1

Initial Consonants

- For initial consonant sounds S. missed, go back to the LWR lesson in *Skill Book 1* where the initial consonant sound is taught. Refer to the chart titled "Skills Introduced in Skill Book 1" at the beginning of the *Teacher's Manual for Skill Book 1.*

- In *Focus on Phonics-1,* use the section on Beginning Sounds and Letters, the Beginning Sounds Worksheets, and the Tests for Beginning Consonant Sounds.

- Using syllables made up of a consonant plus a vowel, have S. try to identify the syllable that begins with the same consonant sound as the first syllable you say. (You need not confine yourself to short vowel sounds.) For example:
  T: Which begins with the same sound as /do/ — /di/ or /fa/?
  S: /di/.

Final Consonants

- For final consonant sounds S. missed, go back to the *Skill Book 1* lesson where the final consonant sound is taught. Refer to the chart titled "Skills Introduced in Skill Book 1" at the beginning of the *Teacher's Manual for Skill Book 1.*

- In *Focus on Phonics-1,* use the section on Ending Sounds and Letters, the Ending Sounds Worksheets, the Review of Beginning and Ending Sounds, and the Tests for Ending Consonant Sounds.

- Using syllables made up of a vowel plus a consonant, have S. try to identify the syllable that ends with the same consonant sound as the first syllable you call. For example:
  T: Which ends with the same sound as /ab/ — /ib/ or /ag/?
  S: /ib/.

BLENDING: Level 2

If S. had difficulty with blending, then before beginning *Skill Book 2,* you should do some work with one-syllable regularly spelled words with short vowel sounds.

It will be easier for S. to begin blending sounds if you start with a few words having only consonants that are *continuants.* That means that the sound can be continued or sustained. Some examples are *f, m, n, r, s, v, z.* (Use *r* only as a beginning sound.) Some words you might work with are:

fan	fuss	mom	miss	rim	Sam
fin	fuzz	man	mess	ram	sun
fun		men		run	van

Demonstrate to S. how to blend sounds. Write the word for S., and say the individual sounds while pointing to each letter. For example, using *fun,* you would say: /f/—/u/—/n/. Say the sounds more and more quickly until they are blended to make the word *fun.* Have S. repeat the process.

Go on with words that have the same continuants *(f, m, n, r, s, v, z)* at the beginning but other consonants at the end. Then go on to words that begin or end with any consonant. If S. has trouble with these, have him say the beginning consonant and the vowel together and then add the final consonant. For example, to blend *pet,* have him say /pe/ and then add /t/.

CONSONANT BLENDS AND DIGRAPHS: Level 2

- For initial or final consonant blends and digraphs, refer to the chart titled "Skills Introduced or Reinforced in Skill Book 2" at the beginning of the *Teacher's Manual for Skill Book 2* for specific blends S. missed.

- Use *Focus on Phonics-2B: Consonant Blends* for work on initial and final consonant blends and digraphs. Use the table of contents to find the practice pages for the specific blends S. missed.

WORD RECOGNITION: Levels 1-4

For words that S. missed on the Student Reading Profile—or for any words being learned—use any of the following activities:

- List words S. missed. Read them with S. several times. Then have S. read them alone.

- For each word that S. missed, write a short sentence using the word. Have S. find and circle the word in the sentence.

- For each word S. missed, have S. dictate a sentence. Read back the sentence you've written; then have S. recall the sentence as you point to the words. Underline the target word, and have S. say it.

- For a word S. read incorrectly, write the word next to two similar words. For example, if S. missed *shop,* write it along with *ship* and *stop.* Name the word S. missed, and have S. point to that word.

- Have S. make flash cards of the words he or she missed. Then help S. practice the words by going over the flash cards.

- For Levels 2-3, help S. practice reading words which have a pattern similar to that of the word S. missed. Patterns might consist of the vowel + final consonant(s), or of the beginning consonant(s) + vowel. Refer to the chart titled "Skills Introduced or Reinforced in Skill Book _____ " at the beginning of each LWR teacher's manual for lessons in which particular spellings for vowel sounds are taught. Also, note whether words S. missed had particular beginning or ending consonant blends or digraphs, endings, prefixes, or suffixes, and find the places in LWR where these are taught.

- Have S. keep a pocket notebook of new words being learned. Together, think of words having similar spelling patterns, and write those on the same page as the original word. For example, for *glass* similar words might be: *glad, pass, grass.*

- For a word S. missed, write the word down, then divide it into syllables (e.g., *physical: phys i cal*). See if S. can now figure out the word. If not, write it out phonetically (e.g., *fiz i cul*). See if S. can figure it out. Return to the original word, and discuss various aspects of the word, comparing it to your phonetic spelling (e.g., in *physical,* the *ph* is sounded /f/ like *f*. Also, the *y* and the *i* both have the sound /i/).

- *Focus on Phonics-2A: Short Vowel Sounds, Focus on Phonics-3: Long Vowel Sounds,* and *Focus on Phonics-4: Other Vowel Sounds and Consonant Spellings* may be used with their corresponding LWR skill books. *Focus on Phonics-2B: Consonant Blends*—which also includes digraphs—may be used at any time after *Skill Book 2.*

PARTS OF WRITTEN LANGUAGE: Level 1
Identifying Sentences

With S., discuss what sentences are, and try to discover his source of confusion about them. Also, give S. more practice with identifying sentences. The punctuation section of page 23 of the *Teacher's Manual for Skill Book 1* is also helpful.

Identifying Paragraphs

- After reading the story in Lesson 6 of *Skill Book 1,* go over the Story Review section in the teacher's manual, page 48.

- With S., discuss what paragraphs are, and try to discover his source of confusion about them. Then give S. more practice identifying paragraphs. Use books, newspapers, form letters, magazines, and so on.

Capitalization

As you go through Lessons 6-10 on capital letters in *Skill Book 1,* draw special attention to the use of capital letters on names, at the beginning of sentences, and in the abbreviations *Mr.* and *Mrs.*

Punctuation

At the *Skill Book 1* level, S. is expected only to *recognize* the purpose of the punctuation marks listed below and to respond to punctuation marks by reading sentences orally with the proper intonation. S. is not expected at this point to *produce* written sentences using these punctuation marks correctly. That comes gradually as S. progresses through the skill books.

— A sentence ends with a period.
— A question ends with a question mark.
— An exclamation comes at the end of something said with excitement.
— Quotation marks set off what someone said.
— The ending -'s means *belongs to.*

- Check the "Skills Introduced in Skill Book 1" chart at the beginning of the teacher's manual for places where the punctuation marks are introduced and explained. As you read stories in *Skill Book 1* with S., you may call attention to punctuation marks at any time to reinforce their purpose.

- Go over the mistakes S. made in Student Reading Profile 1. Talk about the punctuation rule that is involved for each item missed.

- Have S. read sentences or selections from *More Stories 1,* using punctuation marks as guides to verbal expression: a louder tone for an exclamation point, a conversational tone for quotation marks, a rising tone for a question mark, a short pause for a comma, and a longer pause for a period.

WORD PARTS

Substituting Beginning Consonant Sounds or Vowels: Level 2

Teach items S. missed in Student Reading Profile 2. Say the missed item and ask S. to separate the sounds. For example, for *stop,* S. would say: /st/- -/o/—/p/ or /s/—/t/—/o/—/p/. Point out the letters in the first word that are the same as the letters in the second word. Say both words, and have S. tell what sound in the second word is different. Now have S. write the second word.

Endings: Levels 2 and 3
Compound Words: Levels 3 and 4
Contractions: Levels 3 and 4
Suffixes: Level 4

- Refer to the "Skills Introduced" chart at the beginning of the LWR teacher's manual you are working in for particular endings S. is having difficulty with and for compound words, contractions, and suffixes.

  If S. is having difficulty with suffixes, you might want to work on prefixes also, particularly if words with prefixes gave S. difficulty in the Word Meanings section of Student Reading Profile 4.

- Refer to the table of contents in the Focus on Phonics books for exercises on particular endings, compound words, contractions, and suffixes. Also, look in the teacher's editions for appendixes of additional compound words and words with endings.

WORD MEANINGS: Level 4

- Refer to the "Skills Introduced" charts at the beginning of the *Teacher's Manual for Skill Book 4* for places where words that mean the same (synonyms) and words that mean the opposite (antonyms) are taught.

- Have a conversation where a word S. missed is used prominently. If the word is *chef,* you could discuss various jobs in restaurants. Have the printed word in front of S. for S. to see and study as you both talk about it.

- In Student Reading Profile 4, in the section on words that mean the same, note whether some of the student's wrong answers were opposites. If so, he may actually know the word meanings but may sometimes lose his concentration or answer impulsively.

- Also, note whether any of the words S. missed contained prefixes or suffixes. If so, refer to the "Skills Introduced" chart in the *Teacher's Manual for Skill Book 4* to locate places where these are taught.

- For words missed, have S. use both the original word given and its synonym (or antonym) in sentences.

COMPREHENSION: Levels 1-4

- A student who does not achieve mastery on comprehension might be centering his or her attention on recognizing words. If your student did not achieve mastery, ask him or her to read for meaning. Also, when you ask your student to read something, suggest particular information you'd like him to find, for example: "Read this story to find out the names of the uncle and aunt."

- The stories in the skill book of the appropriate level may be used, along with any oral follow-up questions in the teacher's manual or written questions in the skill book. You may ask additional oral questions as needed.

  Also, look through the Checking Progress and Meeting Individual Needs sections of each lesson in the teacher's manual for additional ideas.

- Have S. read single paragraphs from the skill book or the More Stories book for the level you are working on. After S. reads a paragraph, ask questions about what the paragraph said (e.g. "What is the name of Mr. Oliver's pup?") Allow S. to look back at the paragraph at first. If S. does well with the first few paragraphs, give S. practice with not looking back at the paragraph when you ask questions. If S. has a lot of difficulty with understanding the meaning in paragraphs, work on single sentences instead.

- Have S. read various short selections. After reading each, have S. tell, without looking back at it, what the selection said. If S. has a lot of trouble with this, shorten the selections to two or three sentences. For example, S. reads: "Joe's daughter is a runner. She'll be running next Tuesday in the track meet." T. says: "Tell me, in your own words, what you just read about." S. answers something like: "Joe's daughter is going to run in a track meet."

- Have S. read short selections. After each, ask questions about content. For example, if a sentence says, "Carol works in a bank," you might ask, "Where does Carol work?" Allow S. to look back at the selection, and have S. write the answers. If you want to write out your questions for S., try varying the form of your questions. Typical forms of comprehension questions are multiple choice, true/false, fill in the blanks, and answering questions with short answers or complete sentences.

- If S. has difficulty with sequence of events, write out summary statements of key events in the story on separate slips of paper, and have S. arrange them in the order in which they happened.

  It may also be helpful to call the student's attention to the way that time expressions and other transitional phrases like *before that* or *later that day* help us to relate events in the story to one another in time. If a story you are working with is particularly rich in such expressions, have S. underline them.

PRACTICAL READING AND WRITING: Levels 3-4

- Go over the Reading for Living sections of lessons in *Skill Book 3* or *4*—whichever you are working in.

- Bring in some real-life items similar to those in the Reading for Living sections and go over them with S.

- Help S. write down a recipe he or she knows, write a short letter, write a want ad, etc. Discuss each step during the process.

- Go over various applications and forms. Those from your student's actual life situation—such as job applications—make particularly good lessons. Ask questions about the forms to check understanding. (Note: If you have S. fill out the forms, allow him to make up facts to protect confidentiality.)

- S. may need some practice in skimming. Many kinds of practical reading materials are not read word for word from start to finish. We skim to find particular items that we are looking for. You might bring in some want ads for household goods and ask S. to skim for any that mention tables, and put a check mark beside them. Similarly, in ads for used cars, S. might skim for all that are below a certain price.

- If S. is particularly interested in a certain kind of practical reading material, you may want to study its specialized vocabulary more intensively—especially at the *Skill Book 4* level. For example, want ads for jobs, rentals, used cars and so on each have their own specialized abbreviations. There is much cooking vocabulary in recipes. Forms often ask for similar information in different ways.

WRITING

Manuscript Writing (Printing): Level 1. Use the Writing Lesson sections of the lessons in *Skill Book 1*.

Cursive Writing (Handwriting): Level 3. Although cursive writing is not covered in the LWR Diagnostic Inventory, you may want to teach it if S. does not have this skill. The *Laubach Way to Cursive Writing* workbook is designed to be used at the end of *Skill Book 3* before *Skill Book 4* is started.

SPELLING: Levels 3-4

- The Skills Practice and Writing sections of lessons in the LWR skill books tend to be especially helpful for teaching spelling.

- For words that S. has difficulty with, say the word slowly, and then have S. say the word. Ask S. to spell the word. If S. still misspells the word, have S. now write it as you say the letters. Then divide the word into syllables and show S. the letter combinations that make up each syllable. Have S. spell each syllable, then the whole word.

- Analyze words that give S. difficulty to see if his misspelling might be caused by not understanding any of the concepts listed below. If so, refer to the

"Skills Introduced and Reinforced" charts at the beginning of the teacher's manual for the skill book you are working in.

— endings
— irregular plurals
— compound words
— contractions
— prefixes
— suffixes

- If you are already using the Focus on Phonics series, it may be used to help a student with minor spelling problems, especially if the teacher will provide additional spelling drills and tests based on the content of the lessons. Some suggestions are given in the teacher's editions for giving more of a spelling emphasis to the instruction.

- If a student who took Student Reading Profile 3 or 4 showed serious deficiencies in spelling, you may want to use the Patterns in Spelling series. This four-book series is designed specifically for adults who read at the third grade level or higher. As its title suggests, the series stresses patterns regularly found in English words. The patterns are composed of syllables, syllable endings, and consonant blends and digraphs. As students work through the program, they become increasingly independent spellers, learning not only to spell the words presented in the lessons, but also to predict the spelling of other words that contain the same sound patterns.

The diagnostic/placement test for this series will help you to determine which spelling skills your student has mastered and which ones still need to be addressed. This test will also help you to place your student in the proper workbook.

Book 1: Patterns with Short Vowels
Book 2: Patterns with Long Vowels
Book 3: Patterns with Consonant Blends and Digraphs
Book 4: Patterns with Other Vowel Sounds